# ĤOUSEKEEPING

## 101

### Detailed Guide To
### Ultimate Housekeeping

BARBRA ELIZABETH BURNEY

Balboa Press books may be ordered through booksellers or by contacting:

Balboa Press
A Division of Hay House
1663 Liberty Drive
Bloomington, IN 47403
www.balboapress.com
1 (877) 407-4847

Because of the dynamic nature of the Internet, any web addresses or
links contained in this book may have changed since publication and
may no longer be valid. The views expressed in this work are solely those
of the author and do not necessarily reflect the views of the publisher,
and the publisher hereby disclaims any responsibility for them.

Any people depicted in stock imagery provided by Getty Images are
models, and such images are being used for illustrative purposes only.
Certain stock imagery © Getty Images.

ISBN: 978-1-9822-3229-0 (sc)
ISBN: 978-1-9822-3230-6 (e)

Library of Congress Control Number: 2019910923

Print information available on the last page.

Balboa Press rev. date: 08/02/2019

BALBOA
PRESS
A DIVISION OF HAY HOUSE

This book offers detailed instructions with pictures, guidelines, an organizational planner, a scheduling list, tips, tools, and cleaners for the housekeeper to maintain the cleanliness of a home. Contract option included. I have also outlined where hidden smells could be lingering in places un-attended.

# CONTENTS

# INTRODUCTION

*P*rofessionals dress appropriately at all times to avoid giving off wrong signals. Scrubs are a comfortable cleaning uniform. Your personal hygiene will be noticed and will speak volumes about you. Clean closed-toed shoes. Strive for support in every area.

Your customer will notice how clean your vehicle is, and may insist on helping you put things in your vehicle.

Everyone has different needs. Take into consideration their budgets, ages, and disabilities. Do not do anything that you are not qualified to do. Ask what the duties of the day will consist of. Acceptance is adjusting to their ways and routines. Remember that you are in their world now. Pay attention to their habits and accommodate as needed. Visitors may drop by unexpected and interrupt where you are working.

Evaluation of which rooms are used the most by who you are cleaning for is important because a family, a couple, or a single person all require different things. Look through the house and evaluate each room to each customer. Assess before starting by checking for anything needed that may not have been mentioned or forgotten. Take into consideration that tedious cleaning is time consuming.

Report to customer any leaks right away. Call attention to necessary repairs. Do not concern yourself with things that will make you liable for damages.

Anyone Sick and contagious, (customer, housekeeper, children) needs to be reported so you don't pass it along to others.

Pets are like peoples' children. Try to remember the pet's name and ask if the vacuum hurts their ears or if anything else upsets them so you won't upset the customer or get bitten.

When you are in public representing your customer, be professional at all times. What you do for them is confidential and should never be discussed with anyone else. Attitude is everything.

Focus on their needs. Your personal business is not theirs. Leave your issues at home and do not offer information about your private life. It is their wants that you are to help with, not what you think they need. It is not a control issue. It is their trust in you they are looking for. Coins are not yours to keep if you find them. People will place coins or things just to see if you can be trusted. Work as if you are on camera.

This is far more than a routine processing and filing job. Assisting people with their individual needs requires a different kind of attention. There can be emotions attached to the people you are cleaning for, so make sure this is something you can deal with.

If appropriate, ask if there are any numbers that you will need in case of emergency. Keep a detailed planner with mileage and income for taxes, customers keys, and alarm codes in a safe place.

Never mind attitudes – only mind your own. People deal with life in many different ways. Do your job to the best of your ability and leave the rest to God.

# CONTRACT

Be clear about what you will do and what you will not do. If you do summer-time outside windows (heights Yes or No) make it understood which months are too hot for you to be outside. Outside chores are a different rate than inside chores. Do you house-sit animals? Yes ___ No ___. Do you clean nick-knacks/what-nots? Yes ___ No ___. Do you clean curio cabinets with collectibles? Yes ___ No ___. Housekeeper not responsible in any way, shape, form, or fashion for breaking anything asked to be cleaned (customer **Initials**).

Set an hourly rate $_____, which may be different for certain customers due to their needs. Charge by the job $_____, half day $_____, or full day $_____. Cancellation fee $_____. Let them know if you drive a distance so you can calculate in for your mileage _____ or the time _____ it takes to drive from your home to theirs. If you have two half-day customers, let them know that their times must remain the same.

Weekly and monthly rates are not the same because there is more to do once a month. Let the customer know there will be a minimum payment for your time and your drive especially if you are accommodating them with mid-day hours. Do not allow an assumed fee. Never quote over the phone. Customer rates and needs differ.

Customers should respect what you do for them as well as you should respect the privilege of getting their trust to work in their home.

Customers are liable for any unfriendly animals that show a tendency toward biting and should put the animal away to avoid paying a doctor expense. (customer **Initials**).

Some customers will have cameras set up in their home, so always work like you will be on camera. Any recordings made may not be made public in any form (customer **Initials**).

Ask your customers for a 24-hour cancellation notice and if they will let you know of any extended times that they may not need you so you can apply your time elsewhere.

Expect holidays to come with cancellations. Ask your customer if they plan to have you clean for them after the holidays.

Accommodations: Hot water, heat and air conditioning.

You may have a list of reputable references to offer for the things that you do not want to do. For instance: outside windows, shampoo carpets, iron, sew, fireplace, etc.

Housekeeper is not responsible for potential FIRE HAZZARDS: (customer **Initials**)

Built-up lint trapped in the bottom of the dryer lint filter. Faulty wiring.

Washer/Dryer lint behind appliances and built up in duct.

Refrigerator lint on the backside and underneath.

Nothing around hot water heater or air return vent/s.

Heaters clear of lint/dust bunnies and debris.

Hoarding to extreme. Etc.

# CONTRACT

Print Customer Name
Address
City, State. Zip
Mobile Number

**Sign** Customer Name


Print Housekeeper Name
Address
City, State. Zip
Phone Number

**Sign** Housekeeper Name

Any recordings made may not be made public in any form (customer **initials**).

References upon request.

Cc: two-page contract for customer and housekeeper.

# ORGANIZATION PLANNER

*I* have laid out the detailed instructions from room to room. It is totally up to each customer's wishes what is to be done. A home is much easier to maintain after the detail work has been done. It takes a lot more time to incorporate a little detail here and there and usually shows slow progress. A notebook of the detail work and dates done is helpful.

There are weekly, monthly, quarterly, biyearly, and yearly things to be done in each home. Regular things may not get done if there is not pay allotted for time needed for extra work incorporated. Pay is different for each time slot of detail cleaning. Most likely, other than regular cleaning will need to be scheduled on a different day unless each cleaning day that is incorporated with a little extra detail is compensated in a different amount of pay.

There are items to be cleaned from each detailed room if you so desire to go room by room with each detailed room being a different price. Most customers desire a general cleaning with the detail cleaning only done at their discretion. It is up to the customer to choose what is to be done at the time the customer wants or needs it done. A general cleaning item or two can be left to clean another time if customer wants to replace it with a small detail cleaning item.

Please give your housekeeper as much in advance notice as you can to accommodate your needs. Sometimes other customers will comply with changing dates with you, but not always.

Some housekeepers will not do what others will. We are all not comfortable doing everything. We are all servants of God, but respect goes both ways.

WEEKLY usually consists of cleaning bathrooms, dusting, sweeping/vacuuming, mopping.

BI-WEEKLY the same, but with some kitchen items such as refrigerator, stove top, microwave, wipe down appliances, garbage disposal, clean sinks, etc.

MONTHLY could consist of extra items in the kitchen needing attention such as cabinets, drawers, baseboards, etc.

QUARTERLY detail oriented in most rooms, baseboards, blinds, mostly where hidden smells occur.

BI-YEARLY lighting, oven, inside windows, etc.

YEARLY consists of Spring-cleaning detail and organization.

Summer work times may differ from Winter work times.

It is customer preference as to what and when certain cleaning is done and depending on agreed hours to be worked. Each customer has different desires for their homes. Keep in mind that as a housekeeper, you will not be able to please a customer from time to time. Your housekeeper is here to accommodate you, just as you are expected to pay for your accommodations.

# SCHEDULING LIST

*for inside cleaning*

## RESIDENTIAL

**SPRING CLEANING:** (Yearly) Behind and under the washer/dryer/ refrigerator/stove/bed...

**DETAIL:** (Quarterly) Vents, Baseboards, Globes, Light switches, Ceiling fans, Doors, Cabinets, Drawers, Inside Windows and sills, Shutters or Blinds...

**ASSISTANCE:** Laundry, Errands, Driver, Pick-up/Delivery, Shopping, Food Preparation, Gift Wrapping, Organization, Packing...

Before and after Holiday assistance, Family gatherings, Parties...

MOVE-IN/MOVE-OUT CLEANUP

MARKET-READY DETAIL

REGULAR-BASIS CLEANING

## COMMERCIAL

Blinds, Pictures, Seats/Chairs, Under Tables, Window ledges, Ceiling fans, Doors, Vents, Baseboards, Thresholds, Globes, Light switches

Bathroom Detail, Fitting rooms, Kitchen, etc.

Before and after Holiday cleanup, Employee/Family gatherings, Parties, Business Functions, etc.

# TOOLS and CLEANERS

Disposable medium to heavy duty Nitrile Gloves. Kitchen Grout Brush and Bathroom Grout Brush. Scrub Brushes with bristles that extend over the plastic tip of brush to reach in corners. Swivel Tile Grout scrub brush with extension handle. Under-appliance brush. Small delicate paint brush. Toilet bowl brush with under-rim brush attached. Swiffer 360 with extension handle. Swivel Dust Mop. Bona Dust Mop. Bucket, Squeegee, Cotton and T-shirt Rags, Step Ladder, Hand Brush or Corn broom, Broom, Dust Pan, Mop Bucket and Mop (other than sponge), Vacuum with attachments. Permanent marker. Furniture sliders that can be put underneath furniture legs to be moved easier for cleaning behind and under.

SOS Soap Pads, Heavy-Duty Degreaser, Green Scotch-Brite Scrub Pads with no sponge, Magic Erasers, Comet with Bleach, Bleach, Clorox cleaner with Bleach, Scrubbing Bubbles, Old English regular and Dark Scratch-Cover, Easy-Off Oven cleaner, Window cleaner with Ammonia or Vinegar and newspaper. Bona for wood flooring. Multi-purpose cleaners are not as preferable as cleaners for specific items.

**Cleaning Supplies:** Know what is on hand and what will be needed before your next cleaning. Bring supplies in case your customer forgets to pick them up.

Do not use Oil-based cleaners on ceiling fans or wood blinds. Oil-based cleaners may attract more greasy dirt. Diluted Murphy's Oil Soap cleans well unless a degreaser is needed.

Philips and Flat-head screwdrivers, Putty knife, Razor Blades with holder. Q-Tips. Toothpicks. Safety pins. (depending on the extent of detail)

Extra clothes and shoes (optional)

If shopping for your customer, shopping fees are applicable.

# ROOM ORDER OF CLEANING

Bathrooms 1st Kitchen 2nd Living Room 3rd Dining Room 4th Bedrooms 5th Utility Room 6th.

Always clean bathrooms first because you will have to use the facilities also.

Start oven to auto-clean and laundry early depending on the amount of laundry needed to be done as well as the dishwasher so laundry and dishes can be put away before you leave.

Evaluation of which rooms are used the most by who you are cleaning for is important because a family, a couple, or a single person all require different things. Look through the house and evaluate each room for what may need to be done for each customer.

Sweep off ceiling vents and dust from walls. Dry-wipe everything off 1st. On top of cabinets,

*Top of Cabinet*

vanity light and bulbs, top ledge of mirror, top of door and molding, top of the shower ledges, counter top, dust on cabinets, drawers, and door. Wipe down grimy doors and knobs. Use grout brush for around Jacuzzi jets. Fill water over jets after cleaning to release soap scum build-up. Sweep baseboards and floor to remove hair, lint etc.

# HIDDEN SMELLS

Clean Toilet next. With a permanent marker, write "TOILET" on the grout brush so it will not be used for anything else. Wipe tank and handle. Floss with rag underneath where the tank sits on the toilet and underneath bottom of tank.

Start with lid down and use the grout brush to clean in between and around where the lid and seat screws to the toilet

*Toilet screws on lid*

*Underneath Snaps*

*Toilet Snap Covers*

The buttons that keep the lid off of the seat; the buttons that keep the seat off of the toilet bowl; In the grooves where the lid is attached to the seat; In the grooves underneath the seat.

With grout brush, scrub in and around the screws that hold the toilet on.

Clean urine accumulated around the cap that covers the bolt holding toilet to the floor and urine around base of toilet on the floor. Clean the black grime under toilet bowl rim with toilet bowl brush.

*Barbra Elizabeth Burney*

*Under Toilet Bowl Rim*

Discard gloves. Place cleaning rag in washer. Plastic, wooden, and worn out toilet seats absorb urine.

Urine splatters on the side of the bathtub/shower curtain if next to toilet, on the baseboards and wall where the toilet paper is attached, behind the toilet, toilet bowl brush holder, trash can, and magazine rack if next to toilet. Discard gloves. Place cleaning rag in washer.

With wet rag, wipe top ledges of shower and shower head, around knobs, and underneath faucet, overflow drain cap, and around bottom of tub/shower drain.

*Inside And Underneath Shower Drain*

Clean shower walls, underneath shower bar, and underneath the bottom of shower door where soap scum collects. Clean shower door and squeegee door to help prevent hard-water spots. Clean bathtub. Bathroom door grime. If removable, clean sink stopper with grout brush.

*Sink Stopper*

then around the insides of the drain. If not removable, pull up on stopper and scrub around underneath with grout brush.

Drain holes in sinks can be cleaned with a grout brush or a toothbrush and work best to get around faucets and into corners.

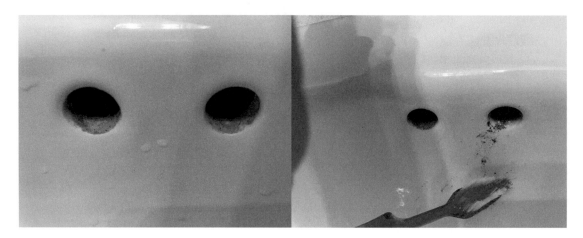

*Sink Drain Holes*

Grout brushes with a plastic tip extending over on the end of the grout brush will **not** allow you to get into the corner completely with the brush.

Clean around the tops of faucet handles with grout brush. Remove and clean underneath the lids of the "Hot & Cold-water knobs and inside knobs also.

*Water Knobs and Underneath Knob Covers*

Floss in between and around faucet handles with a cleaning rag.

*Under Faucet Knobs*

Clean splatters from walls around the sinks; sides and underneath counter tops, towel and toilet paper holders; light fixtures and door knobs. Clean sink and grout around the outside of the sink. Clean mirror. Shake out rugs, sweep again then mop.

# TIPS

Do not leave a bleach cleaner on the rubber gasket around the faucet or on any surface.

*Faucet Gasket*

Always spray a cleaner on the cleaning rag instead of any surface. A bleach cleaner sprayed on the toilet will leave white-streak stains.

Barbra Elizabeth Burney

# KITCHEN DETAIL

Sweep off vents. Use a cleaner on a rag if corroded with greasy dirt. Wash the bottoms of the top row of cabinets where food splashes underneath. Wash grimy doors and knobs. Sweep baseboards and floor to rid of hair, food, etc. Wipe off the bottoms of the furniture legs to rid of accumulated dirt that will leave streaks on floor after mopping.

## MICROWAVE

Wipe out microwave, clean microwave door and digital facing, clean handle, top, sides, underneath, cord, and back of microwave.

## GARBAGE DISPOSAL

While running hot water, insert grout brush inside disposal. With one hand partially covering the top of the disposal, move grout brush up and down while going around insides to clean, also pivoting the grout brush up underneath and around the bottom of the rubber in the disposal. After cleaning, with water running, turn on disposal to rinse away debris.

## SINK

Use a wet grout brush to clean around faucet gasket, around base of spray nozzle and in spray nozzle holes. Floss around faucet handle/s with a wet rag if grout brush will not fit in grooves to clean. If faucet handle tilts upward, clean food grime from underneath, then swivel to the left and to the right. With grout brush, clean crevice around the end of the sink faucet that is handled most to move from one side of the sink to the other. Also, with a wet grout brush go around the outer edge of the sink (where sink sits in the counter) to remove residue, then wipe clean with a wet rag. Scrub sinks with a moistened SOS soap pad, or use comet with bleach and a non-scratch scrub pad.

# REFRIGERATOR

Clean around and inside of grooves of all rubber seals around doors of freezer and refrigerator. With grout brush, scrub grime from crevice in handle of refrigerator door.

*Seam in frig handle*

Wash handles, front, sides, and top of refrigerator. Wipe out any food droppings in freezer and freezer compartments. Neatly stack items back in the freezer when taken out or moved around. Wipe out inside refrigerator, drawers, and compartments in the door. Sweep off or clean grime from the bottom grate of refrigerator and sweep floor.

Roll out refrigerator and dust the back of refrigerator, back and sides of the walls, all the baseboards. Wash sides of refrigerator, sweep and mop under.

# STOVE

**ELECTRIC:** Remove electrical burners and wipe off – Do Not put electrical burners in water. Remove pans under electric burners and put pans in dishwater to soak before cleaning with an SOS soap pad. Pull off knobs to soak, then clean under the knobs and the digital face of the stove. If lid raises up on the stove, brace lid with the metal rod inside of stove to hold it up while you wipe it clean of food, clean it with an SOS soap pad, then rinse with a rag. Clean each side and front underneath lid. Clean around and inside each hole that the burners fit in, and wash under the stove lid.

**GLASS TOP:** Remove knobs and soak in dishwater. Clean under the knobs and the digital face of the stove. Wipe off food particles. Scrape all residue from glass top and wipe. Use glass top cleaner to clean. Scrub with SOS soap pad or scotch-brite scrub pad if needed, and rinse with rag.

**GAS:** Remove knobs and gas grates to soak in dishwater. Wipe underneath or clean with an SOS soap pad, then rinse with a rag. Round burner tops are removable to wipe clean, but Do Not put burner tops in water. Clean the digital face of the stove.

Pull out stove and clean the back of stove, back and sides of the walls, all the baseboards. Clean backsplash, Vent-a-hood, top and sides of stove. Sweep and mop under.

*Stove Heat Vent*

## OVEN

First, ask if anyone may have a problem breathing if you start an auto-cleaning oven. Remove anything that may be stored in the oven. Open the drawer that is under the oven to make sure nothing is stored there that will be damaged or explode from the heat. Open a window for ventilation. Do Not have anything sitting on the stove (or cleaners nearby) while oven is on cleaning mode, because the temperature is very hot. Remove nickel-plated oven racks before starting the oven to auto-clean. Wipe away any food particles that may be left in the oven so it won't start on fire. The panel will show the recommended settings – just start. Allow several hours for cooling of oven. Wipe out oven, then clean up any residue on floor.

## DISHWASHER

Wash off the door, controls, handle, top, sides, and bottom, of dishwasher. Scrub inside if corroded with soap residue. Put all dishes in the dishwasher. Some pots and pans will need to be washed in the sink with an SOS soap pad because some pots and pans will tarnish when washed in the dish washer. Turn on the dishwasher and set on heat dry before you start cleaning the kitchen. Put the dishes up before you leave.

## APPLIANCES

Move small appliances away from walls or out of corners that are sitting on counter tops and wash behind and under where appliances were. Wipe off cords. Some appliances may require the use of a grout brush, or Q-Tips, or even toothpicks to detail clean.

## LIGHTING

If there is a fluorescent lighting cover in the kitchen that needs to be cleaned, ask the customer if they would like it to be cleaned if reachable with customer's ladder. For other lighting, dust light bulbs while cool. Some bulbs will have to be removed before globes can be taken off so globes can be washed inside and out either in dishwasher or by hand. Wash all light switches, wall plug-ins, and door knobs.

## DRAWERS

Remove items from each drawer. Use a vacuum attachment to rid drawer of debris. Wipe drawers from corner to corner with damp cloth.

Use a grout brush to get in corners if needed. Remove silverware from silverware holder and wash holder with dish washing liquid.

## CABINETS

Diluted Murphy's Oil Soap works well to clean *Wood* cabinets and drawers. A spray cleaner with bleach will clean some *White*-painted cabinets. Put degreaser on a rag if cabinets or handles are corroded with greasy dirt.

## BASEBOARDS

Some baseboards will require a bucket of water and the use of a grout brush to remove built up dirt from the corners. Some white-painted baseboards may need a spray cleaner with bleach or mixed with water to remove built up dirt from corners. Some baseboards may need a degreaser or mixed with water depending on how corroded with greasy dirt the baseboards are. Grime build-up on floor around door trim.

## PANTRY

Separate and organize all jar and can goods, pastas, and snacks together with oldest date in front. Chips and crackers have clips or ties on them. Wipe off sticky bottles that may cause ants etc. Wash shelves in pantry. Throw out rusted can food or cans that are swelled.

# TIPS

Start the auto-cleaning oven as early as possible in the morning, due to high temp cleaning, if having to clean oven in mid-summer. Open a kitchen window for ventilation. Turn down the AC if having to clean in hot weather.

Sweep up any residue from appliance cleaning to ensure that it is not embedded into the tile grout, tracked throughout the house, or to eliminate scratching of wood flooring, and to keep from creating floor markings to be cleaned.

Floor cleaners to ratio of water for certain floors is very important. A sticky residue will be left on the floor if too much of a cleaner is used. Always ask the customer what kind of floor it is, and also their preference of cleaner. If concerned, Do Not take chances – just use a mop and warm water. After mopping, look for mop strings left behind stuck under legs of furniture etc. After mopping some floors (when the floor is dry) sweeping may be needed again because of the particles from the mop.

# HIDDEN SMELLS

Under sink or pantry may be where potatoes and onions are stored. If rotted vegetables were thrown away, check for drippings that were not cleaned up. Leaks can cause a musty smell under sinks. In-cabinet trash receptacle.

Garbage disposals will gather residue from food. Scrub underneath the rubber, around the sides, and bottom with a grout brush and/or a scrub pad using a degreaser.

The corners of the baseboards in the kitchen where greasy build up accumulates from cooking. Kitchen blinds and curtains and sticky kitchen counter items.

The splatters on the walls/door where the trash can is. Vent-A-Hoods may have built up greasy dirt on the filter screens and on the back-splash.

Grime around the door of the dishwasher. Food/spills between the stove, counter, refrigerator and underneath both refrigerator and stove.

Food corroded on refrigerator handles and in cervices between handle and door. Black mildew around the rubber of the refrigerator doors and built up food and dirt on the bottom vent screen.

Baked on food in the oven. Around the kitchen faucets. Between counter top and kitchen sink.

*Grime around Sink and Counter*

Kitchen sink stoppers. Under and around the lids of hot and cold-water handles.

Gently shovel out ashes from the fireplace, and sweep up any access from fireplace brick ledges. Sweep off ceiling vents and ceiling cobwebs. Dry dust ceiling fans. Sweep off door moldings, tops of doors, cobwebs behind the doors, panels in doors, and cobwebs in corners of living area. Wipe down grimy doors and knobs. Sweep baseboards and floor. Vacuum, if carpet is in the living area. Use a cleaner on a rag if ceiling vents are corroded with greasy dirt. If ceiling fans need to be washed, diluted Murphy's Oil Soap is a good cleaner for wood ceiling fans. If ceiling fans are corroded with greasy dirt, use a degreaser on a rag, then rinse degreaser from ceiling fan. Dust in door-panel corners may require use of a grout brush. Use a broom or a brush to sweep the return-air vent if in living area. Dust in baseboard corners may require use of a grout brush.

## LIGHTING

### BLINDS

Turn Vinyl or Wood blinds down and wash in between each blade from *top-to-bottom* on each side and in the middle, then wipe dust from strings and cords. Turn Vinyl or Wood blinds up and wash in between each blind from *bottom-to-top* on each side and in the middle, then wipe dust from strings and cords. Vinyl blinds sometimes can be taken down and soaked in a bathtub of water if needed. Do not soak vinyl blinds in any type of bleach cleaner because it will eat the stings into. Wood blinds cannot be submerged in water.

### CURTAINS

If customer requests, certain curtains can be washed on the delicate cycle. Drapes should be taken to the cleaners. Sheers should be dried on the "air only" cycle or hung to dry immediately out of the washer.

# WINDOWS

Wipe the tops of windows where the window locks. A grout brush may need to be used on the locks. Wash trim around each window pane. Wash window sills and the window ledges. Put rag in washer. Clean inside windows.

# DUSTING

Sweep off door moldings, tops of doors, cobwebs behind doors and in corners. Dry wipe pictures, decor on walls, and furniture if excess dust. Dust top ledges of window coverings. Dry-wipe all window ledges. Panels in doors. Dust behind and under all furniture – vacuuming or sweeping underneath if furniture is too heavy to move. Start at the top of wood furniture and dust to the bottom, underneath the bottom edges, around the legs and feet of furniture. Wash wooden-arm chairs. Dry wipe in the creases of couch and chairs. Remove seat cushions from couch, loveseat, and chairs to vacuum under cushions. Flossing with a rag helps to clean any furniture that is tedious to clean. Polish furniture.

Vacuum or sweep and mop floors.

# DINING ROOM DETAIL

Sweep off ceiling vents. Use a cleaner on a rag if corroded with greasy dirt. Dry wipe chandelier & chain clean of dust. Sweep baseboards and floor.

## LIGHTING

Wash the parts of the chandelier that need cleaning and the bulbs while cool.

## BLINDS, CURTAINS, WINDOWS, DUSTING

Wipe off table and any particles out of the dining chairs. Dry-wipe underneath the bottoms of each chair leg and table leg. Diluted Murphy's Oil Soap works well with removing grime from wood dining chairs. Wash off the table and table legs. Wash each entire dining chair. Wash underneath the bottoms of each table leg and chair leg. Some antique furniture may need Old English. The corners of the baseboards may require a grout brush to remove dust. Sweep and mop.

# BEDROOM DETAIL

Sweep off ceiling vents and ceiling cobwebs. Dry dust ceiling fans. Sweep off door moldings, tops of doors, cobwebs behind the doors, panels in doors, and cobwebs in corners. Clean stairway rails. Sweep baseboards and floor. If ceiling fans need to be washed, diluted Murphy's Oil Soap is a good cleaner for wood ceiling fans. Dust in door-panel corners and baseboard corners may require use of a grout brush.

## LIGHTING

Dust lamp shades and bulbs in lamps while cool.

## BLINDS, CURTAINS, WINDOWS, DUSTING, FLOORS

### CLUTTER ORGANIZATION

Shoes: Box-up or stack-up shoes laying in the bottom of the closet. Stack up boxes neatly with labels outward. Shoes can be separated by season.

Clothes: Neatly arrange clothes in closet. You may first start out with putting all shirts together and all pants together, or you may want winter clothes separated from summer clothes. Align clothes where they are all facing the same way.

# UTILITY ROOM DETAIL

Sweep off ceiling vents and lint on walls. Sweep off door moldings, tops of doors, cobwebs behind the doors, panels in doors, and cobwebs in corners of living area. Sweep baseboards and floor. Dust in door-panel corners and baseboard corners.

*Dryer Lint*

# LIGHTING, BLINDS, CURTAINS, WINDOWS, FLOORS

**Laundry:** Wash what is necessary first to remake beds if you are washing mattress pads etc. If you are cleaning and shopping for your customer, you may want to have clothes dry and hung up before you shop so they don't wrinkle in the dryer.

**Linens:** Neatly fold and rotate sheets, towels, etc. when washed as not to accumulate a musty smell.

# ABOUT THE AUTHOR

I have been doing Residential & Commercial Cleaning since 2003. I have always enjoyed helping people. I like a challenge and a sense of accomplishment. Throughout the years, I have become sensitive to each individual's needs. We are all servants of God. To be able to help others with my service not only helps them, but allows me to feel good about being able to help with each person's needs to the best of my ability.

Printed in the United States
By Bookmasters